D1638445

"If you, like me, struggle with discouragement over your weaknesses, you need to read this book. We all long to be admired for our strengths, yet we all find ourselves 'beset with weakness' (Heb. 5:2). Does this mean we're stuck living with discouragement? No! There is an escape to joyful freedom. Dr. Packer knows the way. Walking us through 2 Corinthians, he shows it to us so that we, like Paul, can 'boast all the more gladly of [our] weaknesses.'"

Jon Bloom, President, Desiring God Ministries; author, *Not by Sight: A Fresh Look at Old Stories of Walking by Faith*

"Even the title of this book flies my heart straight to Jesus, kindling afresh my desire to see him as he is. I'm reminded each day that only God's strength can sustain and empower me for service, yet I'm tempted to crave worldly strength. *Weakness Is the Way* emboldens those beset with weaknesses by means of the truth that our human frailty becomes real spiritual strength in and through Christ alone. This is 'life with Christ our strength.' How could we ever want to live any other way?"

Gloria Furman, Pastor's wife and mother of four; cross-cultural worker; author, *Glimpses of Grace*

"I often tell students that biblical 'wisdom' is the product of knowledge, time, and experience, all woven together by deep devotion to the living God. Dr. Packer gives us wisdom in this reflection. Weakness in our culture is hidden, denied, rejected, and avoided at all costs. But admitting it and walking in it are indispensible to biblical faith. Dr. Packer wisely alerts us to how the love of money undermines "the way of weakness" in the modern world! He winsomely weaves into this reflection deep and abiding Christian hope. Our culture sells us self-reliance. God says, 'Rely on me!' Dr. Packer leads us on this path, and I, for one, am grateful for his wise guidance."

Michael S. Beates, Dean of Students, The Geneva School; author, *Disability and the Gospel: How God Uses Our Weakness to Display His Grace*

"Dr. Packer has written a wonderful book about 2 Corinthians that illuminates the varied and various connections between the gospel of Jesus Christ and the Christian life; the power of the gospel and the weakness of the Christian; faith and money; and the present and the future. The exposition that this Christian statesman presents is informed first of all by a penetrating interpretation of the text of Scripture and a consistent theological and Christocentric focus, but also by examples from his own rich life and much else, ranging from C. S. Lewis to cartoons and films. Every Christian should read this book."

Eckhard J. Schnabel, Mary F. Rockefeller Distinguished Professor of New Testament Studies, Gordon-Conwell Theological Seminary; author, *Paul the Missionary*

Weakness

IS

THE WAY

Weakness

IS

THE WAY

LIFE WITH CHRIST
our STRENGTH

J. I. PACKER

ivp

INTER-VARSITY PRESS
Norton Street, Nottingham NG7 3HR, England
Email: ivp@ivpbooks.com
Website: www.ivpbooks.com

First published 2013

British Library Cataloguing in Publication Data
A catalogue record for this book is available from the British Library.

ISBN: 978-1-84474-871-6

Typeset in the United States of America
Printed and bound in Great Britain by Ashford Colour Press Ltd,
Gosport, Hampshire

*Inter-Varsity Press publishes Christian books that are true to the Bible
and that communicate the gospel, develop discipleship and strengthen the
church for its mission in the world.*

*Inter-Varsity Press is closely linked with the Universities and Colleges
Christian Fellowship, a student movement connecting Christian Unions
in universities and colleges throughout Great Britain, and a member
movement of the International Fellowship of Evangelical Students.
Website: www.uccf.org.uk*

My special thanks
go to
Steven Purcell,
whose renewed invitation
to Laity Lodge sparked my theme;
Lane Dennis,
who pressed me
to publish my material;
Scott Barber,
who made sense
of my messy manuscript.

Contents

1

About Weakness

Guide me, O Thou great Jehovah,

Pilgrim through this barren land.

I am weak . . .

WILLIAM WILLIAMS

The Strong and the Weak

In *The House at Pooh Corner*, the second of A. A. Milne's enchanting collections of Winnie-the-Pooh's adventures, we meet fussy mother Kanga, who deems it vital that, whatever else he does, her happy-go-lucky, into-everything offspring Roo should regularly take his strengthening medicine. Why? To grow up strong, of course. And what does that mean? Strength is physical, moral, and relational. Strong people can lift heavy objects, stand unflinchingly for what is right against what is wrong, lead and dominate groups, and in any situation, as we say, make a difference. Strong people carry personal weight, which, when provoked, they can effectively throw around. Strong people win admiration for their abilities and respect for their achievements. Kanga wants Roo to be strong, as other parents want their children to be strong, and as commandants and coaches want those they instruct to be strong—strong, that is, in action.

This is the way of the world, and from one standpoint it is God's way too, as the following exhortations show:

- God to Joshua, whom he was installing as Moses's successor: "Be strong and courageous" (Josh. 1:6–7, 9), said three times for emphasis.
- Paul to the Ephesians, preparing them for spiritual warfare: "Be strong in the Lord and in the strength of his might" (Eph. 6:10).
- Paul to Timothy, encouraging him for the pastoral role to which Paul has appointed him: "Be strengthened by the grace that is in Christ Jesus" (2 Tim. 2:1).

Clearly, it is proper to aim at being spiritually strong and improper to settle for being anything less.

But now look below the surface. Why were these exhortations necessary? Answer: to banish, if possible, the sense of weakness that was there before. It is likely that Joshua, listening to God, and Timothy, reading the words of Paul, were feeling panicky deep down. To follow up Moses's ministry as Israel's leader and Paul's as a church planter were two tremendous tasks; it would be no wonder that neither man felt up to the job. In other words, they felt weak. And there is no doubt that in relation to their assignments they really were weak, and had they not found strength in God, they would never have got through.

For what is weakness? The idea from first to last is of inadequacy. We talk about physical weakness, meaning that there is a lack of vigor and energy and perhaps bodily health so that one cannot manhandle furniture or tackle heavy yard jobs. We talk about intellectual weakness, meaning inability for some forms of brainwork, as for instance C. S. Lewis's almost total inability to do math, and my own messiness in that area. We talk about personal weakness, indicating thereby that a person lacks resolution, firmness of character, dignity, and the capacity to command. We talk about a weak position when a person lacks needed resources and cannot move situations forward or influence events as desired. We talk about relational weakness when persons who should be leading and guiding fail to do so—weak parents, weak pastors, and so on. Every day finds us affirming the inadequacy of others at point after point.

A *Peanuts* cartoon from way back when has Lucy asking a glum-looking Charlie Brown what he is worrying about. Says Charlie, "I feel inferior." "Oh," says Lucy, "you shouldn't worry about that. Lots of people have that feeling." "What, that they're inferior?" Charlie asks. "No," Lucy replies, "that you're inferior." As one who loves witty work with words, I plead guilty to finding this exchange delicious. But some, I know, will find it a very weak joke, unfeeling, unfunny, and indeed cruel: vintage Lucy, in fact—no more, no less—mocking Charlie's gloomy distress and implicitly endorsing his lugubrious self-assessment. It illustrates, however, how easily those who, rightly or wrongly, think themselves strong can rub in and make fester the sense of weakness that others already have. If people who feel weak did not very much dislike the feeling, the joke would not work at all; and if people who at present have no sense of weakness were more careful and restrained in the way they talk of others and to others, the world might be a less painful place.

Often linked with the sense of weakness—sometimes as cause, sometimes as effect—is the feeling of failure. The memory of having fallen short in the past can hang like a black cloud over one's present purposes and in effect program one to fail again. Christian faith, prompting solid hope and promising present help, should dispel all such fears and expectations, but does not always do so, and the encouragement that one Christian should give to another who needs it is frequently in short supply.

The truth, however, is that in many respects, and certainly in spiritual matters, we are all weak and inadequate, and we need to face it. Sin, which disrupts all relationships, has disabled us all across the board. We need to be aware of our limitations and to let this awareness work in us humility and self-distrust, and a realization of our helplessness on our own. Thus we may learn our need to depend on Christ, our Savior and Lord, at every turn of the road, to practice that dependence as one of the constant habits of our heart, and hereby to discover what Paul discovered before us: "when I am weak, then I am strong" (2 Cor. 12:10). But I run ahead of myself.

Paul and the Corinthians

Our present purpose is to take soundings in 2 Corinthians to illuminate the truth just stated—that the way of true spiritual strength, leading to real fruitfulness in Christian life and service, is the humble, self-distrustful way of consciously recognized weakness in spiritual things. This is clearer in Paul than in any other New Testament writer, and it is clearest in 2 Corinthians, because there, more than in any other of his letters, he is writing out of a situation in which, as we would say, he is up against it.

The Corinthian church was more unruly, disorderly, and disrespectful toward its founding father than any of the other churches that were born through Paul's apostolic evangelism. The two letters to Corinth that we have show us that the Corinthians had more lessons to learn, and were slower to learn them, than was ever the case with the Ephesians, Philippians, and Thessalonians. Paul had clearly done his best to explain to the Corinthians what apostolic authority is and why they should shape their lives by his teaching, but it is obvious that they were not fully impressed and were not fully serious in doing what Paul said. Paul loved them and told them so, but found that they were not loving him back. Though he invested himself prodigally in their lives, Paul found that other teachers and other teachings were counting for more with them and that he himself was being continually sidelined by comparison with showier performers. A quick survey of the story so far will make this very clear.

Paul's first visit to Corinth had lasted the best part of two years, probably AD 50–52. Jewish opposition had been strong, but non-Jewish converts were numerous (Luke narrates in Acts 18:1–18). Then, something like four years later, the church sent Paul a letter containing some pastoral queries, to which 1 Corinthians was his answer; and despite needing to rap the church on the knuckles for errors and disorders, he was able at that stage to be basically genial to them. Soon after, however, he had to pay them an emergency visit to look into a disciplinary problem: someone had gone off track and was leading others astray.

Following that visit, Paul sent them a stern letter stating the discipline that should be imposed on the person causing the problem. (Luke, who was evidently composing Acts to a set word length and whose agenda was to trace the triumphant progress of the gospel from Jerusalem to Rome, does not mention any of this, but in 2 Cor. 2:1–11 Paul reviews it in words that show the depth of his distress about it.) Having written thus, Paul was on tenterhooks, wondering whether the Corinthians would take his stern letter seriously or whether by writing it he had lost them.

Out of this anxiety he sent Titus to them on his behalf to see what was happening, and to his delight, Titus reported that the letter had been heeded and the required action taken (see 2 Cor. 7:5–16). But Titus, so it seems, had brought other news too, not so good. "Super-apostles" (2 Cor. 12:11) had descended on the Corinthians and were telling them that much was wrong with Paul's ministry. So Paul resolved to visit Corinth again to deal with the slanders and the slanderers, and he wrote our 2 Corinthians (actually, of course, his third letter to the church) to pave the way.

His purpose for this letter was threefold.

First, he wanted to convince the Corinthians that he loved them, so he opened his heart to them and begged them to open theirs to him (6:11–13). Throughout the first six chapters he highlights the pressures he has been under (near death at Ephesus, 2 Cor. 1:8–10; constantly afflicted, 4:7–18; thought mad, 5:13; exposed to bad conditions and bad treatment, 6:4–10; and see 11:23–33). He shows the sincerity of his ministry, he says, by enduring these things, and clearly he hopes that knowledge of them ("all for your sake," 4:15) will confirm the Corinthians' respect for him.

Second, he wanted to ensure that by the time he arrived, the Corinthians would have completed their collecting of the promised amount for him to take to Jerusalem for poor relief. Christians in Jerusalem were destitute and needed financial help urgently, and Paul had for some time been collecting money from the Gentile churches he founded to present to these needy brothers, thus cementing Jewish-Gentile Christian fellowship in a practical manner. When he reached Corinth, he would be on his way to Jerusalem and hoped to pick up the Corinthian contribution at that time to take with him along with the rest of the money. In chapters 8 and 9, his tone changes to one of pastoral admonition as he writes about all of this.

Third, he wanted to counter the influence of the intruders who sought to turn the Corinthians against him. They had been calling him "weak" to express their contempt for him (10:10). Changing his tone again to one of apostolic rebuke, Paul pleads guilty as charged, but declares that when he is weak, then he is strong, and promises that if necessary he will display his Christ-given strength in dealing with gainsayers when he arrives (12:20–13:4).

The Weak Made Strong

No doubt it was the critics at Corinth who prompted Paul to dwell so directly and fully on his weakness as he wrote this letter. His stress on the providentially appointed hardships of his ministry shows that the relative weakness of his position in both the church and the world has been in his mind all along. So too does his expressed uncertainty about his standing with the Corinthians, which led him to qualify his chivvying of them concerning the collection ("see that you excel in this act of grace also," 2 Cor. 8:7) with the almost apologetic words, "I say this not as a command, but to prove by the earnestness of others [which he wants the Corinthians to emulate] that your love also is genuine" (8:8).

In the third section, however, his acknowledgment of the weakness he feels comes to a climax when he reveals that to keep him from pride, "a thorn was given me in the flesh, a messenger of Satan to harass me" (12:7). What was it? we ask. Eye trouble? Disease? Lameness? Evidently it was something physical and painful, or it would not have been called a thorn in the flesh, but beyond this we do not know what it was, nor do we need to. In three solemn spells of petitionary prayer, he tells us, "I pleaded with the Lord [Jesus, the healer] about this, that it should leave me. But he said to me, 'My grace is sufficient for you, for my power is made perfect in weakness'" (12:8–9).

So Paul went unhealed, though not abandoned. Rather the reverse, as he now testifies: "Therefore I will boast all the more gladly of my weaknesses, so that the power of Christ may rest upon me. For the sake of Christ, then, I am content with weaknesses, insults, hardships, persecutions, and calamities. For when I am weak, then I am strong" (12:9–10).

A Personal Postscript

My own recognition that the Christian way of life and service is a walk of weakness, as human strength gives out and only divine strength can sustain and enable, may well be rooted in my youth. A solitary and rather somber child, I had to wear at school, for ten years, a black aluminum patch covering a hole in my head, the result of a road accident, and hence I was unable to play outdoor games. During those years I felt out of most of what mattered, which is of course one form of the feeling of weakness.

This sense of things, sinful as it is in many ways, has hovered in the background throughout my life, and it has certainly been deepened over the past three years by the experience of a hip disintegrating (two years of hobbling and wobbling discomfort, leading to a year of steady but slow recovery from its surgical replacement).

I was told that since the surgery was invasive, its initial impact would be to shock the system—like being knocked down in the street by a truck—and full recovery for mind and body would take time, with creativity (in my case, power to write) at first noticeably in abeyance. During these three years, my firsthand awareness of physical and cognitive weakness has grown, as has my acquaintance with Satan's skill in generating gloom and discouragement. My appreciation of 2 Corinthians has also grown, as I have brooded on the fact that Paul had been there before me, and this little book is the result. Its contents have helped me, and I hope will help others too.

2

Christ and the Christian's Calling

Christ is speaking in me. He is not weak. . . . He was crucified in weakness, but lives by the power of God. For we also are weak in him, but in dealing with you we will live with him by the power of God.

2 CORINTHIANS 13:3-4

Is Paul Crazy?

As we are beginning to see, 2 Corinthians is unlike any other letter that Paul wrote. The others are written to churches that will accept without question all that he says as coming with apostolic authority—Christ's authority, in fact. So in those letters Paul is very much the teacher telling it like it is. But here he is writing to Christians many of whom, he knows, do not respect him as an apostle. He is under suspicion with them of being something of a kook, perhaps a fraud, and so his first task must be to recapture, if he can, their confidence in him and readiness to learn from him.

Paul is not, I think, used to such situations. Certainly, his usual confident, logical flow in unfolding his thoughts is diminished, and there is some to-ing and fro-ing, repeating and going back on himself, as he seeks to achieve persuasiveness. He is a preacher dictating a letter, so naturally he speaks in a didactic fashion; yet all the time he seems to be asking himself what he can say to get under the Corinthians' skin and convince them that he is a person they should love and learn from after all, despite the way the "super-apostles" have put him down.

This needs to be born in mind as we approach the passage that we are to study now, 2 Corinthians 5:6–6:2.

> So we are always of good courage. We know that while we are at home in the body we are away from the Lord, for we walk by faith, not by sight. Yes, we are of good courage, and we would rather be away from the body and at home with the Lord. So whether we are

at home or away, we make it our aim to please him.
For we must all appear before the judgment seat of
Christ, so that each one may receive what is due for
what he has done in the body, whether good or evil.

Therefore, knowing the fear of the Lord, we persuade others. But what we are is known to God, and I
hope it is known also to your conscience. We are not
commending ourselves to you again but giving you
cause to boast about us, so that you may be able to
answer those who boast about outward appearance
and not about what is in the heart. For if we are beside
ourselves, it is for God; if we are in our right mind, it is
for you. For the love of Christ controls us, because we
have concluded this: that one has died for all, therefore
all have died; and he died for all, that those who live
might no longer live for themselves but for him who
for their sake died and was raised.

From now on, therefore, we regard no one according to the flesh. Even though we once regarded Christ
according to the flesh, we regard him thus no longer.
Therefore, if anyone is in Christ, he is a new creation.
The old has passed away; behold, the new has come.
All this is from God, who through Christ reconciled
us to himself and gave us the ministry of reconcilia-

tion; that is, in Christ God was reconciling the world to himself, not counting their trespasses against them, and entrusting to us the message of reconciliation. Therefore, we are ambassadors for Christ, God making his appeal through us. We implore you on behalf of Christ, be reconciled to God. For our sake he made him to be sin who knew no sin, so that in him we might become the righteousness of God.

Working together with him, then, we appeal to you not to receive the grace of God in vain. For he says,

> "In a favorable time I listened to you,
>   and in a day of salvation I have helped
>   you."

Behold, now is the favorable time; behold, now is the day of salvation.

It can safely be said that all who appreciate Paul's apostleship find this section of 2 Corinthians supremely thrilling, indeed overwhelmingly so. The passage is the climax of the first part of the letter, where Paul is baring his soul in order to reestablish trust, love, and responsive rapport between the Corinthians and himself, and to that end he is highlighting his motivation as a servant of God.

Understanding how people tick, as we say, is always fundamental to good relationships with them. Think of husband and wife, and parents and children, for a moment, and you will have no doubt about that. Paul presents himself here as a driven man and indicates what motivations are driving him. The Corinthians, he knows, suspect that the enormity of his energy and enthusiasm for the church-planting work he is doing argues mental unbalance—to put it bluntly, insanity, some form of religious mania.

Paul sweeps the idea aside. "For if we are beside ourselves [the Greek word means, literally, out of our mind], it is for God"—that is, it is between us and him, and no business of yours—but "if we are in our right mind, it is for you" (5:13)—and you must take us seriously. (The plural here, by the way, is not the authorial "we" that is commonplace in English-language literature; it designates Paul and Timothy together, the twosome announced as sending the letter in 1:1. From the start of chapter 3 Paul has been associating Timothy with himself in everything he has said.)

Paul in effect is begging the Corinthians to ask themselves: Is it possible that Paul and his companion are sane after all? Could it be that it is wrong to mock and belittle them? Do we really understand them? Should we not, after all, see them as guides for our faith and life in the way they want us to do? I hope every reader of this book will join the Corinthians in facing up to these same questions.

Paul's Motivations

In any event, Paul is passionate in desiring that the readers of his letter should properly understand him, and he lays himself on the line accordingly. He now explains what drives him in the risky, hazardous, and often pain-laden service of Jesus Christ that has become his life's work. His motivation, he tells us, is threefold. The three operative thoughts are distinct, but they overlap, and blend and bond with each other to form a single rope of response, if I may put it so, to the overwhelming fact of Christ. As a result, we see Christ as God incarnate into weakness, the baby son of a poor Jewish girl; Christ for three years a peripatetic, disruptive social and religious outsider; Christ crucified in weakness as a revolutionary who had become a nuisance; Christ, Paul's loving Sin-Bearer, absorbing divine wrath against him on the cross; Christ now his risen, reigning, returning Lord, his life and his hope.

The three motives are these:

1. Paul wants to give constant pleasure to Christ.

"Whether we are at home [in heaven] or away [still on earth], we make it our aim to please him," Paul says (5:9). Pleasing those who in some sense have your heart—a spouse, a sibling, a child, a friend, a mentor, a benefactor, or whoever—is a demanding occupation. It calls for imagination, empathy, and effort; you have to be aware of their hopes and expectations that involve you, their likes and dislikes, and their sense of the bond between you and them.

Is this a major motive in our own lives, I wonder: always and under all circumstances to please our Lord and Savior? It was so with Paul, and this agenda, then for him as now for us, is demanding. It requires sustained love to Jesus, expressed in adoration of him for all that he is in himself and thanksgiving to him for all that he has done, for the world of lost humanity in general and for us sinners in particular. It requires sustained obedience to all his commands, up to the limits of our understanding of them. It requires constant watchfulness against temptations to self-indulgence, and constant battling against sloth, laziness, and indifference to spiritual issues. It requires respectful and caring treatment of all others as persons created to bear the image of God, and self-denial at all points where self-absorption would conflict with and damp down active neighbor-love. It requires daily holiness, from morning to night, a daily quest for opportunities to bear witness to Christ, and daily prayer for the furthering of Christ's kingdom and the blessing of needy people.

There is joy in laboring wholeheartedly to please Christ, as Paul knew, but there is no denying that, as Isaac Watts put it, "love so amazing, so divine [as Christ's love, supremely displayed at the cross], demands my soul, my life, my all."

2. Paul wants to be found fully faithful to Christ on judgment day.

Paul continues, "For we must all appear before the judgment seat of Christ, so that each one may receive what is due for what he has done in the body, whether good or evil" (5:10). Here we must watch our step, for centuries of misunderstanding have obscured Paul's meaning in this verse and others like it. Paul is not talking about personal salvation as such. He is not hoping for a final justification that would at last be achieved through the merit of his own devoted service, as Roman Catholic teachers, following Augustine, long supposed.

Let it be said, loud and clear: justification, God's definitive declaration on where we shall spend eternity, is a verdict passed the moment we come to a living faith in Christ. When exactly that is must be left to God, who alone can read human hearts to discern when in each case; but, theologically as well as pastorally, it is always right to assure those who credibly profess penitent faith in Christ that through him their prospect of heaven is now divinely guaranteed. The basis for that verdict is nothing that we do by or for ourselves, but the sin-bearing suffering of Jesus for us on the cross, as we shall shortly see.

From the moment of the verdict, it is the Christian's privilege to live in the assurance of future glory with Christ when life in this world ends. Believers can face the close of life without fear, without panic, without alarm, because they know that whatever else changes, they will be with Christ, in Christ, through Christ, being glorified together with Christ, for ever and ever.

But when Paul says, as in Greek he does, that at the final judgment believers' track records (things "done in the body") since they became Christians will in some sense come back to them as their destiny, he is talking about something else: namely, what we label *rewards*, the divine acknowledgment of faithful service rendered. On this, C. S. Lewis is the most helpful thinker I have read. Lewis asks, what is it that a man in love wants when he courts the girl, woos her, and gets engaged to her with a view to marrying her? Answer: he wants more of the relationship with her that he has already begun. He wants the deepest, richest, most satisfying mode of togetherness with her that it is possible for him to have. He wants, in other words, more of what he has already.

Such is Lewis's analogy for understanding what Jesus and the New Testament writers tell us about the rewards that are to come to Christ's faithful servants at the last judgment. The rewards are pictured in terms of privilege, honor, satisfaction, and joy—that is certainly what the images of feasting, crowning, and ruling are all about. And the prospect of being eternally with Christ and seeing his face and his glory is explicitly spelled out (see John 17:24; Rev. 22:4), as is the expectation of reigning with him (2 Tim. 2:12) and being glorified with him (Rom. 8:17).

On the same topic, Paul taught in his first Corinthian letter that on "the Day" (judgment day) fire will disclose whether each individual Christian has built (in the ongoing life of the church, basing everything on Christ the foundation) with "gold, silver, precious stones," which will survive the flames, or with "wood, hay, straw," which will not (1 Cor. 3:12–13). The apostle has in view halfhearted, opinionated, frivolous, arrogant, disruptive people, destructive rather than constructive in their influence, such as become problems in ordinary congregations today. "If the work that anyone has built on the foundation survives," Paul now states, "he will receive a reward"; but "if anyone's work is burned up, he will suffer loss, though he himself will be saved, but only as through fire" (3:14–15) (i.e., as from a burning building, in which the person escaping has to leave everything behind, to perish in the flames). What "loss" the person escaping will suffer in this case is not specified, but Paul is assuring us that though it will not be the loss of salvation, the loss will be real and grievous. The rewards, by contrast, are for faithfully contributing to the worshipping life and loving, outreaching service of the church of Christ.

"Therefore, knowing the fear of the Lord, we persuade others," Paul continues (2 Cor. 5:11). Knowing that he and his colleagues, like every other Christian, must one day give account to God for the way they have served the Savior since their conversion, and being thoroughly solemnized in his heart by awe in face of this responsibility, he with them invests himself wholeheartedly in their God-appointed evangelistic ministry. The word "fear" in this text is the standard Greek term for fear in the ordinary sense of apprehensive anticipation, causing alarm and perhaps panic; but here it is carrying Old Testament overtones of humble loyalty within the covenantal frame of reverent and adoring awe (as when the fear of the Lord is said to be the beginning of wisdom). Alarm and panic are not in view at all.

God, so Paul now goes on to say, takes knowledge of evangelists as they do what they do, and so Paul adds that he hopes the Corinthians take knowledge of Timothy and him in the same way, for he and Timothy and others like them are deadly serious in their ministry. It is, after all, a life-and-death business (see 2 Cor. 2:15–17), and all the practitioners of this ministry look to be respected accordingly by all who are Christ's (5:11). If you accept this and accept us on this basis, Paul goes on, you should be able "to answer those who boast about outward appearance and not about what is in the heart"—in particular, the "super-apostles" who make malicious fun of Paul's sober teaching style, as well as of things he teaches (v. 12).

Which brings us to the final, climactic motive of Paul and of his teaching.

3. Paul is controlled, claimed, driven, directed, set going, and kept going by the love of Christ.

"For the love of Christ controls us," Paul says (5:14). The verb translated "controls" (and "constraineth" in the KJV) means all that is spelled out above. And "love" is *agapē*, virtually a technical term in the New Testament, meaning a purpose of making a loved one great in whatever way that loved one needs to be made great, and doing so by whatever means are necessary to that end. In the verses that follow, Paul will focus on the two great acts whereby Jesus Christ, the lover of our souls, became our Savior, savingly involving those who by faith lay hold of him in a new life that is in truth his risen life in them. "One has died for all, therefore all have died; and he died for all, that those who live might no longer live for themselves, but for him who for their sake died and was raised" (vv. 14–15).

It is sometimes asked whether Christ's death or his resurrection is what directly brings about the sinner's salvation. The answer is both, and to minimize either's importance in relation to the other is to begin to falsify that answer. In other words, Christ died for our sake as our representative and substitutionary Sin-Bearer, and it is one facet of our faith in him to see and think of ourselves as having died with him, in the sense of having voluntarily ended the life we were living in our unbelief. But that is not all. Christ was raised from death for our sake as our forerunner and life-giver, and it is a further facet of our faith in him to see and think of ourselves as having been raised with him in union with him, so that now we participate in his resurrection life in terms of desire, direction, and divine driving energy. When Paul declared that in his ministry he toils, "struggling with all his energy that he powerfully works within me" (Col. 1:29), it is this supernatualizing of motivated service that he refers to.

So now we are different people from what we were; in some respects, certainly, the same, but in other respects decisively and irrevocably changed. Now we are not running our lives independently, as we did before, but responsively, as we allow Christ, who loves us, and the redeeming love he has already shown in saving us, and his loving purpose for our new lives, to impact us in their full strength. And this will continue, in all appropriate ways, to all eternity. Praise God!

Galatians 2:19–20 tells us a similar story about the Christian's transformed identity, as modeled in the person of Paul once more. "I have been crucified with Christ," he writes. "It is no longer I [apart from Christ] who live, but Christ who lives in me. And the life I now live in the flesh I live by faith in the Son of God, who loved me and gave himself for me" (v. 20). "Crucified with Christ" here corresponds to "all have died" in 2 Corinthians 5:14, and "I live by faith in the Son of God" matches "that those who live might no longer live for themselves, but for him" in 2 Corinthians 5:15. What Paul is talking about is a personal life that is new in the sense that it has a new motivation and is under new management, one that brings vision, direction, communion, purpose, and potential that were simply not there before.

The next block of verses (vv. 16–21) further opens up the differences that the active love of Christ has made in the lives of sinful human beings. Verse 16 says: "From now on, therefore, we regard no one according to the flesh. Even though we once regarded Christ according to the flesh [Paul did!], we regard him thus no longer." This is the first difference: a new way of thinking about people. The imparting of new life to believers has permanently changed the inward mind-set that determines their perception, first of the Lord Jesus himself, and then of others. No longer do believers assess others (Christ included!) in purely human, this-worldly terms, asking only how people might best fit in to society around them and what use we might make of them (this is what "according to the flesh" evidently implies). Instead believers see their neighbors as lost souls, without God and without hope, and they never forget that the primary way to help these lost souls is to share the gospel with them.

Verse 17 adds, "Therefore, if anyone is in Christ, he is a new creation. The old has passed away; behold, the new has come." This is the second difference: a new way of existing among people. Union with Jesus Christ, which correlates with one's first significant embrace of and commitment to Jesus as Lord and Savior, involves a fresh exposure to the same creative power that made the world and today sustains it and generates within it the process that produces and shapes each person in the womb during pregnancy. All who have come to faith in Christ know that they are now different persons from what they were before, and from what their peers—fellow Christians excepted—still are, though they often find it hard to say just what the difference is. Here, however, Paul gives them the theology of the transformation that has occurred, namely, that the re-created and unending personal life of resurrection, derived from and shared with the risen Christ, is theirs already.

The Stupendous Exchange

At this point something arresting happens. It is not unique; it happens elsewhere in Paul's writings, sometimes on a grander scale than here—in Romans 5 and 8, for instance, and Ephesians 1–2. Falling into the preacher's regular proclamatory mode of thought as he dictates, Paul breaks into a rhapsodic doxological declaration, or at least indication, of the wide and wonderful range of God's work of grace in and through Christ, which Paul is privileged to make known in its fullness as near universally as he can. The episodes he describes are, if I may put it musically, the sforzandos and fortissimos of his letters, the moments of emphasis that shape the specifics of what he is laying out at each stage.

Here in 2 Corinthians 5, the fortissimo begins at verse 18: "All this [every aspect of salvation mentioned thus far] is from God"—yes, God!—"who through Christ reconciled us to himself and gave us the ministry of reconciliation." Then comes the conjunctional phrase "that is," which introduces an amplified analysis of what this declaration means. I shall discuss Paul's analysis under three heads, focusing on reconciliation, as Paul does, and highlighting in order its meaning, its method, and its messengers.

THE *MEANING* OF RECONCILIATION

Reconciliation is a big word expressing a big idea, namely, all that is involved in turning a state of alienation, hostility, and apartness into a state of intimate, affectionate, harmonious togetherness on a permanent basis. The initial state of enmity and separation was universal and included liability to and expectation of retributive judgment from God the holy Judge for the sins—trespasses, that is, willy-nilly slips and slides into moral pitfalls—that beset and defile each one of us every day of our lives. The new state of friendship with God, now available to all the world, Jew and Gentile together, rests on Christ's acceptance of incarnation in the womb and propitiation on the cross, followed by his resurrection from the dead, plus vocation by the Holy Spirit in the individual sinner's head and heart, and justification of him or her as the decisive word issuing from the holy Judge. My next point will show this.

THE *METHOD* OF RECONCILIATION

Paul says in 5:21, "[God the Father] made him [Jesus Christ, his incarnate Son] to be sin who knew no sin, so that in him we might become the righteousness of God." The key to understanding this amazing statement is to know that in the days before italics and underlining were invented, a writer of Greek might use an abstract noun in place of an adjective to achieve emphasis. Paul does this in Romans 8:7, where the Greek literally reads, "The thinking of the flesh is *enmity* toward God" (ESV renders the word "hostile," which is the adjective one would expect). Paul also does it here, saying that God made Christ "to be *sin*" (meaning, God counted him and treated him as a sinner, sinless though he was), so that we in him (meaning, we who believe and are united to Christ by the Holy Spirit) become "the righteousness of God" (meaning, right relationally with God, recipients of the divine verdict: not penally liable, now or ever, though guilty as charged; and thus accepted and forgiven).

Paul uses the phrase "the righteousness of God" elsewhere, possibly in a different sense, which scholars debate, but this is certainly what it means here in 2 Corinthians 5! The method of God's reconciliation is here revealed, then, as a two-way transfer, or exchange. On the one hand, the Lord Jesus as our substitute took our place and tasted on our behalf the penalty—that is, the death and banishment into hell—that we deserved. On the other hand, we are made sharers of the Father's eternal approval of and pleasure in his always loyal, loving, and obedient Son, who now has borne, and borne away, the sin of the world. Retributive justice has been done, once for all, and just justification—justification, that is, on the basis of justice thus executed—is now ours for the taking.

Well may we speak of this double action on God's part as the great exchange, the wonderful exchange, and, as I like to do for maximum emphasis, "the stupendous exchange." It is overwhelmingly awesome, almost beyond belief. It is holy love in action—the holy love of the Father, who sent his Son into this world to die for our sins; the holy love of the Son, love for everyone whose sins he bore; and the holy love of the Holy Spirit, who works in our hearts to create and sustain the faith that brings the blessing of reconciliation and acceptance home to us as the supreme gift of divine grace.

It is commonly said that the righteousness of Christ is *imputed* to us (that is, reckoned to our account; the word's background is in bookkeeping). This means not that God pretends that we ourselves did and suffered what Christ did and suffered for us, but that our bonding with Christ by faith and his bonding with us by the Holy Spirit entail that we share forever the status and position that are his by virtue of who he is and what he has done for us. In English society, a commoner who marries a Lord thereby becomes a Lady, and one who marries a Duke or a Prince becomes a Duchess or a Princess, simply by virtue of who her husband is; his dignity now embraces her, so that hers now matches his. In verse 21 the Father's present and ongoing embrace of his incarnate Son as perfectly righteous, to be honored accordingly, embraces us with him, for his sake, by virtue of what he has done for us. This, then, is the divinely devised method of our reconciliation, as Paul sets it forth.

THE *MESSENGERS* OF RECONCILIATION

Paul speaks repeatedly of the messengers of this reconciliation. Observe the following statements:

> God . . . gave us the ministry of reconciliation . . . entrusting to us the message of reconciliation. (2 Cor. 5:18–19)

> We are ambassadors for Christ, God making his appeal through us. We implore you on behalf of Christ, be reconciled to God. (v. 20)

> We appeal to you not to receive the grace of God in vain. (6:1)

That Paul speaks here of the gospel-preaching, church-planting task that God has given him and Timothy in relation to the Corinthians is too obvious to need discussion. But clearly their role and service of ambassadorship for Christ is not, in Paul's thinking or God's planning, confined to the citizens of Corinth. Paul, we know, sees himself as called to be a church-planting pioneer taking the gospel to towns in Asia Minor, in Greece, and as far west as Spain. And clearly, too, Paul does not imagine that he and Timothy are the only gospel messengers in existence. How wide and inclusive, then, is the category of gospel messengers, "ambassadors for Christ" as Paul calls them?

Christ's Great Commission, to go and disciple all nations, was given to the apostles as representing the whole church that was to be, and what Paul writes here should surely be seen as fitting into this larger frame. So, just as all Christians should share Paul's threefold life motivation, as reviewed above, so all Christians should see themselves as sharing the church's calling to make Christ known with a discipling purpose as far and as wide as we can. We are all called to trust, love, honor, worship, and serve Christ, and to practice neighbor-love in all its forms, of which evangelism is one. The church everywhere is called to be a missional community as well as a doxological one, and all Christians are called to pull their weight in both aspects of its ongoing life.

Weakness and Vocation

Now, what has all this to do with the way of weakness, which is what this book claims to be about? How does it bear on the problem of weakness, which we focused on right at the start? Let us see.

I described weakness as a state of inadequacy, or insufficiency, in relation to some standard or ideal to which we desire to conform. As has been indicated already, it takes many forms. There is physical weakness, which keeps us from excelling in sports; there is weak health, which makes us vulnerable to all sorts of diseases; weak capacity limits us as employees, business people, and entrepreneurs; weakness of memory keeps us from becoming top-notch teachers or managers; weakness of character unfits us to be leaders, parents, trainers, team captains, and perhaps team members too; and so on.

Subjectively, the sense of being weak, which the weak yet intelligent person can hardly avoid, generates feelings of inferiority—the Charlie Brown syndrome—and of uselessness and worthlessness, along with consequent gloom and depression—not at all happy feelings to live with. The sense of weakness casts a cloud over one's existence. In this fallen world, where original sin in the form of pride, ambitious independence, and deep-level egocentricity has infected everyone, we all crave to be admired for strength in something, and the expectation that it is not going to happen makes one feel like a punctured balloon and plants bitterness in one's heart. The gospel message, however, which we have been reviewing in this chapter, first calls on us all to be realistic in facing and admitting our sinfulness, our weaknesses, our actual transgressions, and our consequent guilt before God; and then it addresses us, in God's name, substantially as follows:

Look to Christ as your loving Sin-Bearer and living Lord. Embrace him as your Savior and Master. And then in his presence resolve to leave behind the old life of conscious self-service, marred as it was by bitterness, self-pity, envy of others, and feelings of failure, in order that you may become his faithful—that is, faith-full—disciple, living henceforth by his rules under his care.

Love Christ, in unending gratitude for his unending love to you. Labor to please him in everything you do. Let his love constrain, compel, command, comfort, and control you constantly, and, like Paul, stop regarding human approval as in any way important. (Earlier he wrote to the Corinthians, "With me it is a very small thing that I should be judged by you . . . . It is the Lord who judges me," 1 Cor. 4:3–4). Live and love the way Paul did before you, and aspiring eagerness will replace gloom and apathy in your heart.

Lean on Christ and rely on him to supply through the Holy Spirit all the strength you need for his service, no matter how weak unhappy circumstances and unfriendly people may be making you feel at present. We have already noticed how, as part of his response to being berated as "weak" by the Corinthians and their "super-apostles," Paul reveals that Christ has set him to live with an unhealed "thorn" (pain, disability) in his body and has told him, "My grace is sufficient for you, for my power is made perfect in weakness" (2 Cor. 12:7–9). It is time now to take to heart his triumphant concluding comment on this aspect of his life situation: "Therefore I will boast all the more gladly of my weaknesses, so that the power of Christ may rest upon me. For the sake of Christ, then, I am content with weaknesses, insults, hardships, persecutions, and calamities. For when I am weak, then I am strong" (vv. 9–10). So lean on Christ, the lover of your soul, as Paul did, and in all your ongoing weakness, real as it is, you too will be empowered to cope and will be established in comfort and joy.

We may, I think, take it as certain that Paul was not by nature or upbringing weakness-conscious in the way that he came to be after putting himself in Christ's hands on the Damascus road and setting out at Christ's command on his apostolic travels. And we should recognize that the fierce and somewhat disabling pain with which Christ in due course required him to live, and which he clearly accepted as a weakness that would be with him to his dying day, had in view less the enriching of his ministry than the furthering of his sanctification. The clues are there: Paul refers to increase of humility in face of privileged revelations (12:7), deepened dependence on

Christ in face of Satanic discouragements and distractions (vv. 7–9), and a robust readiness to welcome whatever other forms of suffering might come his way in the future (v. 10). He demonstrates a sustained recognition that feeling weak in oneself is par for the course in the Christian life and therefore something one may properly boast about and be content with (vv. 6, 9–10). ("Boast" here means, not parade or be proud of in a self-centered way, but highlight when appropriate as a significant, God-given part of one's life.)

In this, Paul models the discipleship, spiritual maturity, and growth in grace that all believers are called to pursue. When the world tells us, as it does, that everyone has a right to a life that is easy, comfortable, and relatively pain-free, a life that enables us to discover, display, and deploy all the strengths that are latent within us, the world twists the truth right out of shape. That was not the quality of life to which Christ's calling led him, nor was it Paul's calling, nor is it what we are called to in the twenty-first century. For all Christians, the likelihood is rather that as our discipleship continues, God will make us increasingly weakness-conscious and pain-aware, so that we may learn with Paul that when we are conscious of being weak, then—and only then—may we become truly strong in the Lord. And should we want it any other way? What do you think?

3

Christ and the Christian's Giving

> Money answers everything.
>
> ECCLESIASTES 10:19

The Money Pitfall

At the close of the classic crime movie *The Maltese Falcon*, a police officer gazes at a statuette, cast in lead in imitation of a prodigiously valuable, jewel-encrusted, falcon-shaped original, the quest for which had triggered the murder and mayhem throughout. He asks, "What is it?" Humphrey Bogart, as Sam Spade, the anti-heroic detective hero, replies, "It's the stuff that dreams are made of." That, surely, is the perfect comment on the deceptive lure of wealth, in all its forms, to the fallen human heart—which is where this chapter must begin.

What is money? A medium of exchange, a resource for getting hold of things you want and sometimes for getting rid of things you don't want, and a means of gaining power and influence in your circle of society. Many view money as a kind of magic: the more they have of it, the more they want; the more doors they expect it to open for them; and, not surprisingly perhaps, the more reluctant they are to part with any of it. The waking dream of ever-greater wealth grips their hearts like a vice. Why? Because, while they think of poverty and limited resources as signs of inadequacy and weakness, they look on wealth as a source of stability and strength.

Our proud hearts shrink from weakness, real or fancied, in all its forms, as we have already noted, and they embrace whatever looks like strength, including the goal and the reality of affluence. The result? Idolatry: we end up worshipping our investments, our possessions, and our bank balance. And God—the transcendent triune Lord who is the Father, the Son, and the Holy Spirit together, the divine team that is currently in action for our salvation—comes a poor second in our loyalty and love.

Jesus saw this and warns us against it, "You cannot serve God and money" (Matt. 6:24). "Money" in the original is *mamōna*—Mammon—a Semitic word meaning not only money as such, but what money is expected to secure for us: things, property, gain, success, and so on. Again, Jesus tells us of the rich man who said to himself, "'You have ample goods laid up for many years; relax, eat, drink, be merry.' But God said to him, 'Fool! This night your soul is required of you and the things you have prepared, whose will they be?'" (Luke 12:19–20). And Jesus replies to the rich ruler, who has asked what he should do to inherit eternal life: "One thing you still lack. Sell all that you have and distribute to the poor, and you will have treasure in heaven; and come, follow me" (Luke 18:22). Jesus meant, quite specifically, "join my disciples trekking with me through Palestine, living by the hospitality people show us, but personally penniless"—a prospect that, unhappily, the rich ruler could not face because his wealth had fast hold of his heart. Paul, we find, warns of the money pitfall in comparable terms: "Those who desire to be rich fall into temptation, into a snare, into many senseless and harmful desires that plunge people into ruin and destruction. For *the love of money is a root of all kinds of evils*" (1 Tim. 6:9–10).

So, what should we do when our basic needs have been met and we still have money in our pockets; when we find that doing whatever it is that we do professionally to earn our living, as we say, and that presumably we think of as service to others and so to God, is actually making money for us; when the business we run is proving profitable, and the money is piling steadily up? Jesus and Paul give the same answer. Use the money, not for yourself, but for God and God's people; use it to spread God's kingdom; use it to help persons in need. See yourself as manager, steward, and trustee of God's funds, honored by the responsibility you have been given but totally accountable to God who gave it to you.

Paul directs Timothy:

> As for the rich in this present age, charge them not to be haughty, nor to set their hopes on the uncertainty of riches, but on God, who richly provides us with everything to enjoy. They are to do good, to be rich in

good works, to be generous and ready to share, thus storing up treasure for themselves as a good foundation for the future, so that they may take hold of that which is truly life. (1 Tim. 6:17–19)

And Jesus crisply exhorts us all, applying to us the lesson of his parable of the dishonest but shrewd manager: "Make friends for yourselves by means of unrighteous wealth [called "unrighteous" here because of the manager's financial shenanigans in the story], so that when it fails [that is, can do no more for you, i.e., when you die] they may receive you into the eternal dwellings" (Luke 16:9).

It was Luther, so I am told, who said that everyone needs three conversions: conversion of the mind to gospel truth; conversion of the heart to embrace the Lord Jesus as Savior and Master; and conversion of the purse, wallet, or pocketbook, the laying of one's money at Christ's feet. The saying is worthy of Luther, who sees to the heart of just about every issue, even if, as I suspect, Luther did not actually craft it. He certainly knew that getting sin out of the driver's seat in relation to our money is one of the most difficult dimensions of the sinner's repentance.

Today, pastors often tell us that when people become Christians, the last thing in their life to be touched by God's transforming grace is regularly their wallet. When directed to commit their time, talents, and treasure to the Lord, giving him financial control starts later, goes slower, and takes longer than does the forming of the other two habits, presumably because the inner resistance is stronger.

A comic strip I enjoyed showed a mother, with a bawling baby in her arms, chatting in the street with a friend: "What's the trouble with baby?" "Oh, he's teething." "And your husband?" (who is sitting on a bench in the background, his open-mouthed agony matching that of the baby). "Oh, he's tithing." Tithing as a life commitment to Christian giving at 10 percent annually is always a good start, but however much it is commended from the pulpit, it is constantly evaded by those in the pew. To motivate generous giving goes against the grain of the fallen human heart, and so it is always hard labor.

So when Paul formed his plan of getting Gentile churches he had planted to contribute to a major collection for the relief of Jewish Christian poverty in Jerusalem, he must have known from the start that the project was a bold one and that convincing success in it—that is, the raising of a worthy sum, one that would demonstrate real love on the part of the Greeks for those who were in Christ before them—could by no means be guaranteed. The project was very much a venture of faith.

Concerning the Collection

The sense in which the Christian life is essentially a pathway of weakness along which God leads us, sustaining and strengthening us for service as we go, is now becoming clear. With regard to tasks and relationships, it is often right, and part of our calling, that we should embrace options in which we may easily find ourselves out of our depth, and in which we know that we cannot hope to succeed without God's help. And with regard to circumstances, it is often the case that in God's sovereign providence unforeseen difficulties arise, throwing us back on the Lord for support and subjecting our faith and faithfulness to very grueling tests. One way or another, God works out in all our lives the baptismal pattern of through-death-into-new-life-with-Christ, which the rite

itself models as under-the-water-then-up-from-under.
And that shows us how absolutely right and on target
William Law was when he wrote:

> Receive every inward and outward trouble, every dis-
> appointment . . . darkness . . . and desolation, with
> both thy hands, as a true opportunity, and blessed
> occasion, of dying to self, and entering into a fuller
> fellowship with thy self-denying, suffering Saviour.
>
> . . . Look at no inward, or outward trouble, in any
> other view; reject every other thought about it; and
> then every kind of trial and distress, will become the
> blessed day of thy prosperity. (*An Humble, Earnest,
> and Affectionate Address to the Clergy* [New-Bedford:
> Lindsey, 1818], 136–37)

When circumstances seem to conspire to make and leave
you weak, Law is saying, Christ always intends that you
should turn to him and find new strength, as we have
already heard Paul tell the Corinthians that he is doing
vis-à-vis his thorn in the flesh. In all of everyone's Christian life and ministry, weakness is indeed the way.

This being so, one way of understanding what is going
on as Paul writes 2 Corinthians, perhaps indeed the pro-

foundest way, is as follows: Paul's central purpose is to make sure that when he reaches Corinth, the collection will be complete for him to take to Jerusalem. Chapters 8 and 9, then, which call for this, are the real occasion for the letter, and the real heart of it. But Paul fears his call for completion will not be taken seriously, partly because his entire apostolic pastorate is under criticism at Corinth, and partly because he fears he alienated the congregation, deep down, first by his severity against the person whose alleged aberrations made necessary the fact-finding visit and sharp letter, and then by his decision not to visit them as early as he planned.

Paul's fear is that the Corinthians will conclude that he is a flighty, unpredictable, self-serving person, as many traveling teachers in those days no doubt were. When the chips are down, Gentiles living in a rough-and-tough Greek port city might not seem to matter much at all to him, save as a cash cow to exploit for the benefit of his fellow Jews. Proper respect for Paul as the Corinthians' founder-pastor would be impossible if that happened, and Paul's anxiety here is fully understandable. So what does he do?

He starts by spending what turns out to be more than half the letter laboring to reestablish the Corinthian's trust in him and, if possible, their affection for him, before he ever mentions the collection. When finally he gets to it, he spends two chapters bending over backwards to encourage and motivate the Corinthians toward generosity. Then, transitioning suddenly for the second time, he rounds off the letter in tones of apostolic authority alternating with crushing testimony, pleading that he be taken seriously now so that there will be no ground for tension when he comes among them again. But for Paul it is really the collection that is crucial all the way, from the letter's first sentence to its last.

Why is the collection so important for Paul? Because when in Jerusalem something like a decade earlier, James, Peter, and John agreed that Barnabas and Paul should go with their blessing to evangelize the Gentile world, "they asked us to remember the poor [in Jerusalem], the very thing I was eager to do" (Gal. 2:10). So for some years Paul, bound by his promise, has been planning poor relief via the Gentile churches that he founded. In 1 Corinthians 16:1–4 Paul prescribes a discipline of setting money aside each Lord's Day for this purpose. A year later, in 2 Corinthians 8:10–11, Paul gently chides his readers for having become irregular and slack in this, and encourages them to finish what they started. For him, as these chapters show, it is very important that the Gentile churches fulfill the undertaking given when the Gentile mission began.

What does Paul actually say about the collection to stir the Corinthians to renewed effort? His points may be summarized thus:

The churches of Macedonia (the Philippians and Thessalonians, in northern Greece) have already excelled in the grace of giving to this good cause, despite their poverty. Paul wants the Corinthians, who excel in so much else, to match them, or do even better (8:1–7). Here, Paul is gently shaming the Corinthians into taking action.

He is not giving a command to them, but expressing a hope for them, that they will give in a way that shows their gratitude to Christ for enriching them through the cross, that corresponds to their earlier commitment and to what the Macedonians have already given, and that is proportional to their measure of affluence (8:8–15).

Here, Paul is vigorously stirring the Corinthians into taking action.

Titus and two other leaders will come to Corinth ahead of Paul to ensure that the collection is complete and ready for him to pick up when he arrives. That way, there will be no risk of embarrassment should Macedonians, to whom Paul has proclaimed the Corinthians' commitment, arrive with him, as they might, and find the Corinthians unready after all. Clearly, Paul is anxious that the whole process of collecting and transporting this gift of money to Jerusalem should be, and be seen to be, smooth, straightforward, honest, and aboveboard, first to last. His anxiety is reasonable enough. For a traveling teacher to collect and then abscond with money would not have been hard in those days; Paul knows this, just as the Corinthians did, and has resolved to make it evident that no such thing will happen in this case (8:16–9:5). Here, then, Paul is dispelling suspicions that could hold the Corinthians back from generous contributions and keep them from taking wholehearted action.

God in his providence will do good to those who become generous, cheerful donors to his cause (9:6–11).

Here, Paul gives practical encouragement to the Corinthians, as believers in God's faithfulness, to express their faith and hope in responsive action.

The Jerusalem Christians will appreciate the Corinthians' generosity enormously, and will express their appreciation by thanksgiving and prayer for them and a desire for closer fellowship with them. So God will be glorified (9:11–14). Here, Paul gives spiritual encouragement to the Corinthians, as units in the body of Christ and devotees of God, to give themselves to God and Paul as the Macedonians had done, and thus to take consecrated action.

It would seem that Paul's pleas succeeded, for we read that he, with a team of eight (the seven named in Acts 20:4, plus Luke the narrator), came to Jerusalem in due course, and "the brothers received us gladly" (Acts 21:17). No doubt the entire collection was delivered to the leadership at that time.

A Primer on Giving

"Primer" is a word that we use to refer to what is first and fundamental in various branches of life, from applying paint to learning languages. (I was taught Latin three-quarters of a century ago from *The Revised Latin Primer*.) I now offer my readers a primer on Christian giving, for which 2 Corinthians 8–9, the main New Testament passage on the subject, provides the raw material.

This, to start with, is the text of 2 Corinthians 9, where all the key principles are directly stated:

> Now it is superfluous for me to write to you about the ministry for the saints, for I know your readiness, of which I boast about you to the people of Macedonia, saying that Achaia [the part of Greece where Corinth was situated] has been ready since last year. And your zeal has stirred up most of them. But I am sending the brothers so that our boasting about you may not prove empty in this matter, so that you may be ready, as I said you would be. Otherwise, if some Macedonians come with me and find that you are not ready, we would be humiliated—to say nothing of you—for being so confident. So I thought it necessary to urge the brothers to go on ahead to you and arrange in advance for the gift you have promised, so that it may be ready as a willing gift, not as an exaction.

The point is this: whoever sows sparingly will also reap sparingly, and whoever sows bountifully will also reap bountifully. Each one must give as he has decided in his heart, not reluctantly or under compulsion, for God loves a cheerful giver. And God is able to make all grace abound to you, so that having all sufficiency in all things at all times, you may abound in every good work. As it is written,

> "He has distributed freely, he has given to
>   the poor;
>   His righteousness endures forever."

He who supplies seed to the sower and bread for food will supply and multiply your seed for sowing and increase the harvest of your righteousness. You will be enriched in every way to be generous in every way, which through us will produce thanksgiving to God. For the ministry of this service is not only supplying the needs of the saints but is also overflowing in many thanksgivings to God. By their approval of this service, they will glorify God because of your submission that comes from your confession of the gospel of Christ, and the generosity of your contribution for them and for all others, while they long for you and pray for you, because of the surpassing grace of God upon you. Thanks be to God for his inexpressible gift!

In light of what this chapter teaches, I shall attempt to answer four questions: (1) What is Christian giving? (2) Why should we Christians give? (3) How should we Christians give? (4) How do the principles and practice of Christian giving bear on our exploration of how apparent human weakness becomes real spiritual strength in and through our Lord?

WHAT IS CHRISTIAN GIVING?

I answer the *what* question with four assertions.

1. Christian giving is both a spiritual gift and a discipline of discipleship to our Lord Jesus Christ.

What is a spiritual gift? Paul's Greek has two label-nouns for identifying any item in this category: *charisma*, meaning a product of the active, communicative, redemptive divine love that the New Testament calls *charis*, and we call grace, and *pneumatikon*, meaning an expression

of the life and energy of the divine person whom the
New Testament calls *hagion pneuma*, the Holy Spirit. A
spiritual gift, a grace gift as we may well describe it, is
essentially a pattern of service in the church that honors
Christ, glorifies God his Father and ours, edifies one's
fellow believers and oneself too, and imparts strength
and maturity to the church as a whole. Some gifts are
abilities that transcend one's natural resources and are
supernaturally bestowed in and through Christ; others
are natural abilities redirected, sanctified, and activated
by the Holy Spirit from within on each occasion of their
exercise. Thus, Paul's intermittent healing powers were
a gift of the first type, while his unflagging powers as a
teacher of gospel truth were a gift of the second type.
Giving, now, is a gift of the latter sort.

In Romans 12:6, Paul writes, "Having gifts that differ
according to the grace given to us, let us use them," and
he proceeds to give examples of this, emphasizing each
time that one use his or her gift in the best way possible.
He speaks of prophesying (i.e., preaching the word of
God), serving, teaching, exhorting, and exercising leadership. Then in verse 8 he comes to this: "the one who

contributes [should do so] in generosity." "Contributes" is a word in the Greek that means "shares" and certainly refers to the sharing of money, as those who have give to meet the needs of those who have not. "Generosity" is a term that also signifies "sincerity," and Paul probably selects it for use here because it always carries overtones of transparent goodwill being expressed.

So giving or sharing or using money to relieve needs is a spiritual gift, and one who gives generously is as truly a charismatic as one who prays for another's healing or who speaks in tongues. Also, giving is a discipline of discipleship to the Lord Jesus. Disciplines do not come naturally, without effort. On the contrary, they are acquired and sustained habits of thought and/or behavior that need constant practice if they are ever to be anything like perfect, and they often involve specific techniques of their own.

Christian virtues, of which generosity is one, are disciplines that Christ commends, commands, and models as life qualities that should mark out all his disciples, that is, all those who have committed themselves to learn his way of living. (The Greek word for "disciple" means learner.)

All spiritual gifts are, from one standpoint, disciplines of discipleship, and if we are not actively traveling the path of generous giving, it will have to be said of us straightaway that we really are weak and deficient in our discipleship to and dependence upon Christ Jesus our Lord—which means that we need, urgently, to change our ways.

2. Christian giving is management of God's money.

When we set ourselves to think about Christian money management, in whatever connection, from buying groceries to supporting missionaries to investing in industry to financing a holiday, the first thing we have to get clear on is that the money that is ours to manage is not ours, but God's. Yes, we have been given it to use, but it remains his. We have it as a loan, and in due course we must give account to him of what we have done with it.

That is the point of the word *stewardship*, which nowadays is in effect the church's label for the discipline of giving. A steward is someone whom an owner entrusts with the managing of his assets. An investment manager is a steward: he has control of his clients' assets in one sense, but his job is to understand and implement his clients' wishes and priorities regarding their use. In the same way, a trustee is a steward: his job is to invest, safeguard, and disburse the money in the trust according to the stated purpose of whoever appointed him.

Society (which Scripture calls "the world") sees each person's money as his own possession, to use as he likes. Scripture, however, sees our money as a trust from God, to be used for his glory. In the Holy Communion liturgy in the Anglican Book of Common Prayer, the collection is offered to God with the words: "All that is in the heaven and in the earth is thine. All things come of thee, and *of thine own have we given thee*" (words taken from 1 Chron. 29:11, 14). Such is the constant biblical perspective. The money that is ordinarily thought of as ours remains God's; we receive it from his hand as his stewards and trustees, and must learn to manage it for his praise.

3. Christian giving is ministry with God's money.

Ministry means service; service means relieving need; need means a lack of something that one cannot well do without. Paul calls his plan of financial help for the

Jerusalem poor "the ministry for the saints" (2 Cor. 9:1) because the poverty of the poor is denying them necessities of life. Paul celebrates, and sets forth as a model, the way in which the Macedonian churches have embraced this mode of ministry, ascribing their action directly to the grace of God. "In a severe test of affliction, their abundance of joy and their extreme poverty"—what a combination!—"have overflowed in a wealth of generosity . . . . they gave . . . beyond their means, of their own accord, begging us earnestly for the favor of taking part in the relief of the saints . . . they gave themselves first to the Lord and then by the will of God to us" (2 Cor. 8:1–5).

The ministry of giving has many goals: spreading the gospel, sustaining the church, providing care for distressed individuals (as the Samaritan in Jesus's story did for the beaten-up, half-dead Jew), and for distressed groups like the Jerusalem Christians, and more. The ministry of giving in all its forms aims to advance the kingdom of God, which becomes reality in human life whenever the values and priorities of Christ's teaching are observed. It goes without saying that in this ministry, all God's people are meant to be involved.

4. Christian giving is a mind-set regarding God's money.

Management and ministry are matters of motivated performance. A mind-set, or mentality as we may prefer to call it, is a characteristic attitude, a habitual orientation, an entrenched desire, and as such a matter of motivation and purpose. Christian giving aims at pleasing and glorifying God and never settling for what is clearly second-best; such, positively and negatively, is the use God means us to make of the money he entrusts to us.

Jesus told the story of a servant who, given a talent to use, did nothing with it beyond hoarding it till he could return it to his master; "wicked," "slothful," and "worthless" are the adjectives his master applied to him (Matt. 25:14–30). Never settling for the fairly good, the possibly good enough, or the not-bad calls for enterprising and imaginative thought, for which the biblical name is wisdom. Giving randomly, without wisdom, is sub-Christian, just as is giving nothing or giving far less than one could.

That raises the question, *how much* should one give? Specifically, should we tithe? Some seem to think that tithing is like paying God rent: when we have given him 10 percent of our income, the rest is ours. But no, it is all God's, and the New Testament nowhere tells Christians to tithe. What Paul tells the Corinthians is not that they should raise their share of the collection by tithing, but that if they give generously to God, he will give generously to them.

> The point is this: whoever sows sparingly will also reap sparingly, and whoever sows bountifully will also reap bountifully. . . . God is able to make all grace abound to you, so that having all sufficiency in all things at all times, you may abound in every good work. . . . You will be enriched in every way to be generous in every way, which through us [as we deliver your gift] will produce thanksgiving to God. . . . they will glorify God because of . . . the generosity of your contribution for them. (2 Cor. 9:6, 8, 11, 13)

Paul's appreciation of the Macedonians for giving "according to their means . . . and beyond their means, of their own accord" (8:3) suggests that his answer to the question, how much should one give? would be, give all you readily, easily, and comfortably can, and then prove your zeal and wholeheartedness for God by giving something more.

In light of Jesus's commendation of the poor widow who put into the temple treasury all she had, it is natural to suppose he too would answer our question by challenging us along these lines. This is certainly how John Wesley was thinking when he told his lay preachers, "Give all you can," and how C. S. Lewis was thinking when he directed a correspondent who had put our question to him, "Give till it hurts." By dint of constant giving, Wesley himself died almost penniless, and Lewis's private charities, so we are told, were huge.

It may be a good idea to practice tithing as a crutch until we get used to giving larger sums than we gave before, but then we should look forward to leaving the crutch behind because now we will have formed the Christian habit of giving more than 10 percent. When the amount to give is in question, the sky should be the limit, and the word of wisdom, "Go for it."

WHY SHOULD WE CHRISTIANS GIVE?

Though the question of why we should give has effectively been answered already, it will be helpful, I think, briefly to pull the threads together and crystallize our answer by taking a leaf out of the book of the Bible teacher who recast Christ's Beatitudes (indicatives about Christian life) as Be-attitudes (imperatives about Christian living). Here, then, are four Be-attitudes that make up my answer to the question.

1. Be grateful to your gracious God.

It has been truly said that in the New Testament the doctrine is grace and the ethic—that is, the prescribed behavior—is gratitude. And the gratitude is prompted by both the knowledge of the grace of Christ in one's head and the power of that grace in one's heart, with Christ as the center of attention at all times in both. "For you know the grace of our Lord Jesus Christ, that though he was rich, yet for your sake he became poor, so that you by his poverty might become rich" (2 Cor. 8:9). Giving to God should ever express unending gratitude for almost unbelievable grace.

2. Be generous to your needy neighbor.

We may properly label grand-scale generosity to someone in trouble "Samaritanship," in echo of Jesus's parable. But we should not forget that he told that story to answer the question, "Who is my neighbor?" And his answer plainly is, any and every person whom you meet, or who confronts you, is your neighbor, whose need, once you see it, you must do your best to relieve. The essence of Christian existence is, after all, a matter not of labeling but of loving, and loving is a matter not of words but of action.

3. Be given to Christ your Savior as his disciple.

Follow the pattern of your Master's lifestyle. Some years back, a popular description of Jesus was "the man for others." More, certainly, must be said than that but, equally certainly, not less. Self-giving, in the sense of devoting all his powers and resources to the service of others, was his hallmark and must be ours too. We are to make good our claim to be Christ's disciples, and to avoid Ananias-and-Sapphira-type hypocrisy, we also must give, and share fully, for his sake, whatever kind of wealth we have.

4. Be a glorifier of God.

Praise, honor, and thank him yourself for all he has given
you. Plan, like Paul, to do and give in a way that will draw
out of others praise and thanks to God. And thus labor
to evoke, and ensure, adoration and appreciation of the
God you yourself appreciate and adore. Generous giving,
in particular, will ordinarily give rise to this effect, as will
all the forms of single-minded obedience and service to
God that others see in us.

Paul is working hard as an organizer, facilitator, and
courier of the collection, but he is not looking for personal
praise. Thanksgiving that glorifies God, by all involved
in the situation, is what he wants to see. Writing in the
slightly stilted style that reflects his sense of the extreme
delicacy of the motivating enterprise that he has in hand,
Paul says that the Corinthians' generous giving

> through us [as proposers and deliverers of the gift] will
> produce thanksgiving to God. For the ministry of this
> service is not only supporting the needs of the saints
> but is also overflowing in many thanksgivings to God.
> By their approval of this service, they [the Jerusalem
> believers] will glorify God because of your submis-

sion [to the claim of their need, as communicated by Paul] that comes from your confession of the gospel of Christ, and the generosity of your contribution for them and for all others. (2 Cor. 9:11–13)

Taking these four Be-attitudes to heart will surely make givers out of the most miserly of us.

Paul's closing words, "Thanks be to God for his inexpressible gift!" (9:15), seem to refer comprehensively to the gift of Jesus Christ to be our Savior and to involve us, with the Corinthians, in the chain-reaction process of generosity, thanksgiving, and fellowship that glorifies God and is in itself an enriching privilege to be part of.

HOW SHOULD WE CHRISTIANS GIVE?

What should be the manner of Christian giving, attitudinally speaking? Let us learn the five points that Paul makes about this.

1. Giving should be voluntary.

Donors must not be put under pressure and stampeded into precipitate and perhaps reluctant action. They must be given space to think out what they are going to do so that their action will express a considered judgment that this is what they ought to do, and in doing it they are doing the best they can in their particular situation to further the kingdom of God, acting, first to last, of their own free will.

In 9:3–5 Paul explains why he is sending three colleagues to Corinth ahead of himself, namely, to "arrange in advance for the gift you have promised, so that it may be ready [when I arrive] as a willing gift, not as an exaction." The Greek word rendered "exaction" regularly expresses ideas of active greed and squeezing out of people donations that they do not wish to give. Paul does not want anyone to give unwillingly, doing it only because the apostle is hounding them for money, and so he makes a point of negating any suspicion to that effect. "Each one must give as he has decided in his heart, not reluctantly or under compulsion, for God loves a cheerful giver" (9:7)—and no giver will be cheerful who wishes that he or she did not have to give at all.

2. Giving should be cheerful.

"God loves a cheerful giver" (9:7). Whence the cheerfulness? The next verse answers that question: "And God is able to make all grace abound to you, so that having all sufficiency in all things at all times, you may abound in every good work." Those who give as generously as they can, with their spirit anchored in this confidence regarding God's future for them, will find a certain exhilaration and lightness of spirit within them as they do it and then reflect on what they have done. Their action has expressed both gratitude to God for his grace hitherto and faith in his faithfulness for time to come, and it should be no surprise when God himself acknowledges this by sustaining in them a happy heart that feels his love. Any readers who make this experiment for the first time will, I think, be surprised to discover how marked the exhilaration can be.

3. Giving should be deliberate.

It should be planned and thoroughly thought out, taking account of all the preexisting financial claims that we are under obligation to meet. Maximal giving must not lose touch with reality and become irresponsible, any more than it should invoke the "Corban" evasion of the Pharisees that Jesus denounced in Mark 7:9–13. "If the readiness is there, it is acceptable according to what a person has, not according to what he does not have," writes Paul (2 Cor. 8:12). Readiness with realism is what he is commending.

4. Giving should be wisely managed.

Paul's anxiety that everything connected with the collection should be, and be seen to be, aboveboard and accountable to all the parties involved is obviously prudential wisdom. So too is the care he takes to ensure that neither he, who has trumpeted to the Macedonians about Corinth's readiness to contribute, nor the Corinthians themselves should be embarrassed by the Macedonians, who have given so freely themselves, now finding that the Corinthians are not ready after all (9:2–5). Paul understands Christian fellowship to require of him, and of everyone else, a threefold relational concern: to trust, to be trusted, and to be found trustworthy. Surely he is a model for us in this.

5. Giving, where possible, should be cooperative.

Common causes, in which people band together to give for a single purpose (like Paul's collection, or a local church budget, or a neighborhood project today), call for giving according to Paul's principle of fair shares: fair in the sense not of all parties giving equal amounts, but of all being equally committed to giving all they can and so helping each other to reach the target (8:10–15). It is a fact that when done on the fair-shares principle, thus understood, giving deepens fellowship wonderfully.

(We should note that Paul makes his fair-shares point in a delicate and roundabout way, like a man walking on eggs. This is doubtless because he knows that the Corinthians know, or if they do not they soon will, that what they promised a year earlier was much more than the Macedonians, whose generosity Paul has praised so highly, have managed to raise. And he is very anxious that no attitudes of rivalry or superiority arise in Corinthian hearts to keep them from enthusing about the project as a venture in all-round Christian fellowship.)

HOW DOES MONEY BEAR ON WEAKNESS?

Finally, what has all this to do with walking the pathway of weakness, which I ventured to identify as the truest Christian life?

We saw at the start of this chapter that fallen human nature puts a very improper, inflated value on money, treating our investments and bank balances as the supreme source of security, status, significance, respect, and influence in society. The world, it seems, sees itself as a place where the rich count and the poor don't, and many Christians appear to have bought into this view. So the more prosperous they become, and the older they get, the harder they find it to contemplate taking the risk—and risk, humanly speaking, it is, of course—of giving generously, year by year, to Christian causes. It is embarrassing to acknowledge that the wealthier Christians become, the less they give, but that is what in many cases seems to happen.

Weakness, however, meaning inability finally to control our life situation relationally, circumstantially, financially, healthwise, and so on, despite all that our therapeutic present-day culture can do for us, will be with us as long as life in this world lasts. Our Lord Jesus Christ lived in poverty through the years of his ministry and, having been despised and rejected, as Isaiah phrased it, he was "crucified in weakness" (2 Cor. 13:4). This tells us what kind of life road we as his disciples must be prepared to travel. Paul, depending on the risen Christ, found strength to live with weaknesses and shows us how to do the same. But our weaknesses will not go away any more than his did, and if we think that money can banish them, we actually add to them by cultivating self-deception. The truth to face here is that we are all called to learn the skill of godly money management and wise Christian giving as Jesus and Paul teach it, and we should be grateful for 2 Corinthians 8 and 9, chapters that give us a head start.

4

Christ and the Christian's Hoping

Blessed be the God and Father of our Lord Jesus Christ!
According to his great mercy, he has caused us to be born
again to a living hope through the resurrection of Jesus
Christ from the dead, to an inheritance that is imperishable,
undefiled, and unfading, kept in heaven for you.

1 PETER 1:3–4

The Quest for Hope

"Where there's life, there's hope" is a deep truth. Deeper,
however, is the converse: "Where there's hope, there's life."
We humans are hoping creatures; we live very largely
on and in our anticipations, things we know are coming
and we look forward to. If the light of hope goes out, life

shrinks to mere existence, something far less than life was meant to be. This is a fact that must be faced.

It was a Headmaster's Conference boys' school, one of England's educational elite, and amid its quite brilliant galaxy of instructors the scholar who stood out was the man we called Bill (behind his back, of course), the headmaster. When I studied Greek and Latin classics at Oxford, I met up with no tutor who could hold a candle to Bill or could teach me half as much as Bill had taught me already. He was a clergyman's son who had retreated from the faith and become a sort of Buddhist.

Decades later, chatting with one of my former pedagogues, I asked after Bill, by then retired and, as I knew, in his early nineties. The reply to my question, based on a recent visit, ran thus (I seem to recall it word for word): "He's very low. I asked him what he was doing these days; all he would say was, 'Waiting for the end.'" Remembering the sharp-edged, upbeat vigor of Bill's mind in his heyday, I felt very sad for him. Buddhism, as we know, does not beget hope. So here was a long-lived man, brilliant in his day, now withering rather than blossoming as he aged. Is that the best one can hope for?

"Hope springs eternal in the human breast," declared Alexander Pope in his usual pompous way, but that is not all the story. For the first half of people's lives, spontaneous hope does indeed spur them forward. Children hope to do this and that when they grow up; teens hope to go places and do things when they have some money; newlyweds hope for a good income, a good place to live, and good-quality children; established couples hope for the day when the children will be off their hands and they are free to cruise, tour, and see the world. But what then? There comes a point at which the elderly and those who, as we say, are getting on realize that of all the things they wanted to do, they have done all they can, and the rest are now permanently out of reach ("life's too short," we say wryly).

Yet life goes on. Today, indeed, people live longer than once they did, but the common experience is that extended and extreme age brings only bleak boredom and a diminished sense of the good life as consisting merely of three meals a day, television to watch, and a bed at night. Whether, as bodily health fades and minds and memories run increasingly amok, any better, more enriching experience of old age is possible is a question that secular social theory has shown itself unable to answer.

But the Bible appears to have an answer.

> The path of the righteous is like the light of dawn,
>> which shines brighter and brighter until full
>>> day. (Prov. 4:18)

> So even to old age and gray hairs,
>> O God, do not forsake me,
> until I proclaim your might to another generation.
>> (Ps. 71:18)

Moses's ministry began when he was eighty. What makes the difference? What does the Bible give us that secular theory cannot match? In a word, hope: hope understood not in the weak sense of optimistic whistling in the dark, but in the strong sense of certainty about what is coming because God himself has promised it. This hope is unique in the fields of both religion and philosophy. The philosopher Kant observed that the question, what may I hope for? is one of the most important questions one can ever ask, but he did not claim he could answer it.

The Bible, however, speaks directly to it, setting before those who are Christ's a destiny that reaches beyond this world to a kaleidoscope of wonders, enrichments, and delights to which it gives the generic name "glory." This destiny is big and exciting, and the New Testament writers show that they felt it to be so. As having something big and exciting to look forward to—a major family holiday, say—will keep children alert and on tiptoe for quite some time before it happens, so the big and exciting future for Christ's faithful disciples that Paul looked forward to undoubtedly kept him at full apostolic stretch through all the adverse experiences to which he alludes in 2 Corinthians.

And do the New Testament writers as a body, with the Lord Jesus himself, expect this promised destiny to bring excitement and awe and amazement and joy into the hearts of all Christian people? The answer is an emphatic *yes*. This then is the prospect, the hope of which the promise is the wellspring, that we are now going to explore.

That leads us to the passage on which we shall be centering our attention, 2 Corinthians 4:5–5:8. Here it is:

What we proclaim is not ourselves, but Jesus Christ as Lord, with ourselves as your servants for Jesus' sake. For God, who said, "Let light shine out of darkness," has shone in our hearts to give the light of the knowledge of the glory of God in the face of Jesus Christ.

But we have this treasure in jars of clay, to show that the surpassing power belongs to God and not to us. We are afflicted in every way, but not crushed; perplexed, but not driven to despair; persecuted, but not forsaken; struck down, but not destroyed; always carrying in the body the death of Jesus, so that the life of Jesus may also be manifested in our bodies. For we who live are always being given over to death for Jesus' sake, so that the life of Jesus also may be manifested in our mortal flesh. So death is at work in us, but life in you.

Since we have the same spirit of faith according to what has been written, "I believed, and so I spoke," we also believe, and so we also speak, knowing that he who raised the Lord Jesus will raise us also with Jesus and bring us with you into his presence. For it is all for your sake, so that as grace extends to more and more people it may increase thanksgiving, to the glory of God.

So we do not lose heart. Though our outer self is wasting away, our inner self is being renewed day by day. For this slight momentary affliction is preparing for us an eternal weight of glory beyond all comparison, as we look not to the things that are seen but to the things that are unseen. For the things that are seen are transient, but the things that are unseen are eternal.

For we know that if the tent that is our earthly home is destroyed, we have a building from God, a house not made with hands, eternal in the heavens. For in this tent we groan, longing to put on our heavenly dwelling, if indeed by putting it on we may not be found naked. For while we are still in this tent, we groan, being burdened—not that we would be unclothed, but that we would be further clothed, so that what is mortal may be swallowed up by life. He who has prepared us for this very thing is God, who has given us the Spirit as a guarantee.

So we are always of good courage. We know that while we are at home in the body we are away from the Lord, for we walk by faith, not by sight. Yes, we are of good courage, and we would rather be away from the body and at home with the Lord.

Upbeat in Weakness

The first thing to note about this passage, and indeed the entire letter, is how extraordinarily upbeat it is. We have seen already that 2 Corinthians exhibits Paul to us at his weakest situationally—consumed with a pastor's anxiety, put under pressure, remorselessly censured, opposed outright and by some given the brush-off, and living in distress because of what he knew, feared, and imagined was being said about him by this rambunctious church at Corinth. We might have expected his sense of weakness in his relationship with the Corinthians to sour him and make him distant and defensive in addressing them. But no, there is no crumpling under criticism, no cooling of pastoral affection; and hope for the future, both here and hereafter, pours out of everything he says at every level. The whole letter is an awesome display of unquenchable love and unconquerable hope. It is Paul's hope, particularly, that concerns us here.

Recent scholarship has highlighted the fondness of biblical writers for what is often called bookending, that is, enclosing what they have to say on particular subjects within opening and closing statements that, in effect, join their voices in speaking of what is spelled out in the territory lying between them, the first statement being introductory to this material, and the second being conclusionary. (In the days before paragraphing and chapter divisions, this was a convenient way of separating and rounding off units of thought. And, of course, it reflects what we humans actually do, and have always done, in our oral communication. When we have something complex and weighty to say, we start with an overall declaration that we then unpack, and we close with a summary statement matching that declaration, which pulls back together and reunites the various threads that our unpacking has separated out. This explains how it is that one can usually get to the heart of a book by skim-reading it, that is, by leaping from the first to the last sentence of every paragraph.)

Observe, now, the bookends between which the essential message of 2 Corinthians is sandwiched. (Let me say here: 12:11–13:14 is a personal afterword about Paul's forthcoming visit, distinct from the matters of substance that he planned out before starting to dictate the letter.

In this respect it is comparable to Romans 15:14–16:27, which follows the closing bookend there too.)

Here is the opening bookend, 2 Corinthians 1:3–4:

> Blessed be the God and Father of our Lord Jesus Christ, the Father of mercies and God of all comfort, who comforts us in all our affliction, so that we may be able to comfort those who are in any affliction, with the comfort with which we ourselves are comforted by God.

This is a far stronger statement than might appear, because the English word "comfort," both as a noun and as a verb, has lost so much of its meaning. When, back in the sixteenth century, it was chosen for the translation of these verses, it meant what the Greek verb means, namely, renewal of strength through encouragement. Today, when "comfort" suggests only some form of cushioning, making comfortable, and reducing pain, it is easy to miss the true thrust of what Paul is saying. Paul is praising God for his endless supply of strength to keep us going and rising to every occasion, and Paul is assuring the Corinthians hereby that though they may think of him as down, he is not out yet.

And now here is the closing bookend, 12:9–10:

[Christ] said to me, "My grace is sufficient for you, for my power is made perfect in weakness." Therefore I will boast all the more gladly of my weaknesses, so that the power of Christ may rest upon me. For the sake of Christ, then, I am content with weaknesses, insults, hardships, persecutions, and calamities. For when I am weak, then I am strong.

Upbeat? Yes—terrifically, wonderfully so. And, as surely is clear by now, the tone and temper of all that Paul writes between the two bookends, topic by topic, is equally upbeat. For all that Paul is writing out of a situation of weakness and, without doubt, a sense of weakness more intense than we meet in any other of his letters, he is not lapsing into self-pity or voicing gloom and doom, but he is expressing his sense of ongoing triumph in Christ in face of all obstacles. And he is declaring his sure and certain hope of glory when his course through this world reaches its end. It is this hope for his personal future—a hope which, to echo Bunyan's Mr. Stand-fast, lies as a glowing coal at his heart—that determines his attitude toward all the pressures of the present, as we are now to see.

Supernaturalized Living

We pick up the flow of Paul's thought at 2 Corinthians 4:7. Speaking on behalf of his ministering colleagues as well as himself, as he has been doing since the start of chapter 3, he contrasts the "treasure" God's servants have with the "jars of clay" they have it in. The treasures are the knowledge of the glory of God in the face of Jesus Christ, the world's now-enthroned Lord; the clay jars are their fragile, vulnerable physical bodies, exposed to every conceivable form of weakness, pain, degeneration, and distress. Paul then proceeds, in 4:8–10, to give the first of his three lists of actual troubles that attend his and their ministry (the others are in chaps. 6, another "we" passage, and 11, where Paul speaks in the first person singular).

In verse 7 he has said that God's purpose in this state of affairs was that "the surpassing power"—the power displayed in their fruitful ministry—might be seen to be God's rather than theirs, and in verses 10–11 he tells us the nature of this power, namely, the resurrection life of Christ. Those who minister the gospel, he says, carry about in their bodies the dying process (that is what the somewhat unusual Greek word means) that Jesus underwent on the cross.

What was that dying process? Pain and exhaustion, with ridicule and contempt, all to the nth degree; a tortured state that would drive any ordinary person to long for death, when it would all be over. But, says Paul, Christ's messengers are sustained, energized, and empowered, despite these external weakening factors, by a process of daily renewal within. So "death is at work in us, but life in you" (4:12). Eventually, however, "he who raised the Lord Jesus will raise us also with Jesus and bring us with you into his presence. For it is all for your sake," to bring you to share in the ever-growing chorus of thanksgiving that gratitude for grace, itself generated by grace, is currently producing "to the glory of God" (4:14–15).

Meantime, however hard the going for the ministers themselves, "we do not lose heart" (4:16, as v. 1). "We are always of good courage" (5:6, 8). While our outer, public self (the person bearing our name that the world knows, or thinks it knows) wastes away, our inner self (we as we know ourselves, and as God knows us) "is being renewed day by day. For this light momentary affliction is preparing for us an eternal weight of glory beyond all comparison" (4:16–17). We are on our way home, and home will be glorious. And contemplating that glory, however inadequately we do it, will brace minds and hearts to resist the weakening effect, the down-drag into apathy and despair, that pain, hostility, discouragement, isolation, contempt, and being misunderstood—and all the rest of the suffering—might naturally have on us otherwise.

Ministers of Christ will keep on keeping on, no matter what. The watching world may well wonder where they find the energy to do so, but the puzzlement of outsiders is no concern of theirs. What animates and propels them is the power of their hope as they "look not to the things that are seen but to the things that are unseen. For the things that are seen are transient, but the things that are unseen are eternal" (4:18).

This is how, by grace, the God of grace supernaturalizes the natural, bodily, mortal life of all who through faith are in Christ, united to him by the Holy Spirit for endless power and joy. God-taught hoping leads to God-given strengthening. When, humanly, we are weak, then in the Lord we are strong. So it was for the apostles and their colleagues two millennia ago, and so it can and should be today for you and me.

Glory

One mark of the supernaturalized life, as Paul depicts it, is the reality of the appearance within it of *glory*—or perhaps I should amend that to "*glories*," for the word "glory" is used in this part of the letter, as elsewhere in the Bible, in three distinct though connected senses. Weight, or weightiness, and consequent grandeur are the ideas at the root of the Hebrew word, and overtones of these ideas are attached to all three uses of the term.

"Glory" refers, first, to what God *shows*, and what shows God to us, namely, his own active presence with self-manifestation to eye or ear or both. In Old Testament times, and in the Old Testament text, the visual aspect of this glory was presented in symbols, principally two: dazzling white light, like that of the sun, such as shone from Moses's face when he had been with God (2 Cor. 3:13), and a huge throne, occupied, such as Isaiah and Ezekiel saw (see Isaiah 6; Ezekiel 1). In the New Testament, by contrast, the awe-inspiring glory is in the face, or person (the Greek word can mean either), of the Lord Jesus Christ, who is God incarnate (2 Cor. 4:6; see John 1:14; 17:5, 24).

Then, second, "glory" refers to what the godly *give* to their God, namely, praise in response to the praiseworthiness that he has shown to them. This is the sense of the word in 2 Corinthians 4:15. The first and second senses meet in the classical Anglican Eucharist, where the Prayer Book has us saying: "Heaven and earth are full of thy *glory*. *Glory* be to thee, O Lord Most High." Praise to the One who is praiseworthy and adoration of the One who is adorable are basic aspects of the love of God with heart, mind, soul, and strength that Jesus identified as the Great Commandment of the law.

Third, by an extension of the first meaning, "glory" points to God's continued transforming work in us whereby "we all . . . beholding the glory of the Lord, are being transformed into the same image from one degree of glory to another" (3:18). This is the glory that God *bestows* on his covenant children, those who have a living faith in Christ and are united to Christ, and in whom the Holy Spirit, the master mason in character building and habit forming, now dwells. Though truly supernatural, the transformation is not in this life physical; it consists, rather, in "the fruit of the Spirit . . . love, joy, peace, patience, kindness, goodness, faithfulness, gentleness, self-control" (Gal. 5:22–23). The Spirit imparts in the heart, as a matter of purpose, the desire for and habit of thus realizing the moral profile of Jesus, which is Christlikeness in the most significant sense of that word.

This process is in fact the first stage of being glorified with Christ, as he has now been glorified, which is the destiny God has appointed for us who believe (see Rom. 8:17, 30). And as the ongoing formation of Christlike character qualities in us is supernatural, so is the cognitive process whereby we come to know the little that we do know about this, and about the further dimensions of God's forthcoming work in our lives. Through this process, which is effected by the Spirit of God through the Word of God, we learn that each of us is a work in progress, inasmuch as "this light momentary affliction is preparing for us an eternal weight of glory beyond all comparison" (2 Cor. 4:17). And we further learn that this work of grace that reshapes us is advanced "as we look [the Greek verb implies an intense, steady gaze] not to the things that are seen but to the things that are unseen. For the things that are seen are transient, but the things that are not seen are eternal" (v. 18). By this kind of looking we come, in the fullest sense, to live.

To speak as Paul does of looking, and looking hard, at what is unseen and at present unseeable sounds paradoxical, but Paul's purpose in speaking this way evidently is to make memorable his summons to the mental and spiritual discipline of sustained thought about our goal of glory. This, he knows, is the best he can do to keep Christian minds and hearts facing in the right direction—that is, forward—so that our hope may fill our horizon and, countering our weakness by adhering to this our source of strength, we may keep on keeping on, traveling hopefully until we arrive; which, contrary to what Robert Louis Stevenson thought, will be the happiest thing imaginable.

Hope Fulfilled

What is it, then, that we have to look forward to? Second Corinthians 5:1–8 sets before us in picture language that aspect of our hope which will counter, cancel, and consign to far-off memory "this light momentary affliction"—bad health, crippled limbs, bodily pains; minds, memories, relationships, personal circumstances all going downhill; insults, cruelties, and whatever else. This hope fills us with wondering joy that everything can be so good. We shall be given a new dwelling place, says Paul, new clothes, and a new home life in the company of our Lord. It sounds marvelous, and so indeed it is. It sounds, in fact, too good to be true, but that is not the case. Let us focus on it as we move toward our close.

Note, first, the *certainty* of what we are about to be told. "We know," says Paul (5:1). How so? Surely, from the words of Jesus, plus, I guess, revelations mediated to Paul directly. In 12:7 the apostle refers to "the surpassing greatness of the revelations"; I presume, though I cannot prove, that what Paul specifically assures us of in 5:1–8 was among them. I proceed on that basis.

Note, next, the *content* of Paul's certainties.

1. We shall be given a new dwelling-place.

Paul begins his unveiling of the Christian's personal hope by talking about the body, telling us of a better body to come. We humans are, as we all know, embodied souls—personal selves, that is, individuals who have been given bodies to live in and live through. Our bodies have three purposes: (1) They are for experiencing realities, which we see, hear, touch, taste, smell, and react to with feelings of all sorts. (2) Our bodies are also for expressing ourselves, which we do through the looks on our faces, the utterances and tones of our voices, the moving of our hands, and the shifting of our posture, thereby showing what is going on inside us. And (3) our bodies are for enjoyment, inasmuch as all life's primary pleasures, eating and drinking and sweet sensations of all sorts, come to us through our bodies. A disembodied life, such as Plato dreamed of, in which the only pleasures are intellectual, would be a far poorer thing than the embodied lives that we are actually living now.

Yet there is a debit side. Paul is a tentmaker by trade, so from one point of view it is not surprising that he should picture the body in which we now live as a tent—a temporary residence. But Paul is a civilized first-century man, a town-dwelling church planter and pastor when he is not actually on the road, so it is not surprising either that he should picture the better body that is in store for us as a house rather than a tent—a permanent, higher-quality habitation into which God has promised that he will one day move us. Tents, when all is said and done, make very vulnerable living quarters. They leak, they get rain-sodden and drip, they let in the cold and the heat, and the earth around, if not the earth inside, becomes muddy, making surface dirt part of the camp experience.

I have camped in a tent (who, these days, hasn't?), and I disliked it very much, though most people, I know, are different and enjoy camping, at least in small doses. But everybody (so Paul assumes, and surely he is right), if asked to choose whether they will live long-term in a tent or in a house, will choose a house, a place, that is, where the limitations and inconveniences of tent life do not apply.

Living in our bodily tents, we groan, says Paul (twice! 5:2, 4), and we have reason to. All sorts of diseases, discomforts, and under-the-weathernesses come our way;

and as we age, the reality, and so the feeling, of our limitations grows and grows. The groaning expresses, on the one hand, intense longing for the bodily house that is to come and, on the other hand, intense frustration (we feel "burdened," weighed down) with the reach-exceeds-grasp and if-only and oh-no-not-that aspects of life as it comes to us in the present. (In these opening verses of 2 Corinthians 5, Paul is of course following on from his testimony to "carrying in the body the death of Jesus" in 4:7–18. Giving that testimony must have left him with a very strongly stirred-up inner ache for the joy of his future heavenly home. This seems to be reflected in the jumpy vividness of the verses that follow. Yet it is clear that in saying "we," "our," and "us" throughout this paragraph, Paul is including all Christians with himself at all points, at least as far as verse 10.)

2. We shall be given new clothing.

Some of Paul's wording as he speaks of what awaits him and his readers is very striking. Thus, he begins by referring to the possibility of his tent being "destroyed" (2 Cor. 5:1). This reflects his awareness that in the ups and downs of his travels, amid various forms of human hostility and with his thorn in the flesh as a constant companion, his life was always at risk and might be ended, suddenly and violently, at any time. And sudden death, as he knew and we know, may similarly overtake any believer. All of us need always to be ready to leave this world, and we can only live well if we are.

Then in verses 3 and 4 we find Paul negating the idea that, having said good-bye to our body, we shall forever be and feel "naked" or "unclothed," in a state of permanent loss. That is not what we want and not what we shall have. On the contrary, what awaits us is possession of a new "house"—a "building from God . . . not made with hands, eternal in the heavens" (5:1). We shall "put on" this house as one puts on a garment over what one is wearing already (an overcoat, for instance, for going out of doors on a cold day). Thus we shall not be "unclothed," but "further clothed" by what God is doing to us; hereby "what is mortal" will be "swallowed up by life" (v. 4).

The metaphors are mixed and a bit blurry, but the basic meaning is clear. Whatever God's work of putting us into our resurrection bodies may involve, and that is more than we can imagine at present, it is not going to be impoverishing but enriching. It will not feel frustrating but fulfilling. And it is already on its way. "He who has prepared us for this very thing is God, who has given us the Spirit as a guarantee" (v. 5). The transforming presence of the Holy Spirit in our hearts and lives (see 3:18) is the deposit or down payment whereby God assures us that this putting-on ("over-coating," as one commentator puts it) is most certainly going to happen.

At this point, as we have already insisted, Paul is pursuing his personal pastoral apologia; his mind is not set in the teaching mode, and he does not tell us everything we would like to know about the destiny he is outlining. In particular, he does not speak to the question, Does our putting-on occur at the moment of death, or is it God's plan that all Christians, starting with the apostles, should wait together till Christ returns publicly to bring about the general resurrection? He seems to imply the latter in 4:14, but then the question arises, How should we conceive life in what is called the intermediate, or interim, state between our death and our resurrection? And that is a question that must be left largely unanswered. We simply do not know, not having been told.

One key thought about it, however, is already before us, namely, that we shall at no stage suffer any sense of loss or impoverishment over leaving our bodies behind. And a second key thought now follows, namely, that from the moment of our death we shall be at home with our Lord Jesus Christ. This is something that Paul looks forward to. "While we are at home in the body we are away from the Lord . . . . and we would rather be away from the body and at home with the Lord" (5:6, 8). All believers should feel that way, for no matter how old or sick we are, thoughts of our future with Jesus will bring fortitude and joy into our hearts. Jesus himself, from his throne, will see to that.

What can we say in positive terms about the trans-formation, or reembodiment, that awaits us, which Paul pictures here as installation in the new house that is henceforth to be our home? Not much, it must be admit-ted, and the positive things are negatives really. In the ideal new house in this world, everything works perfectly and nothing malfunctions, and in our resurrection bodies it will be the same. Jesus, risen, remained recognizable, so we can be sure that when we are "further clothed," the same will be true of us. So we shall know each other and have joy in that knowledge.

Our new body, we may be sure, will match and perfectly express our perfected new heart, that is, our renewed moral and spiritual nature and character. That body will reflect us as we were at our best, rather than as we are physically at the time of leaving this world; indeed, we should expect it to be better than our physical best ever was. The new body will never deteriorate, but will keep its newness for all eternity. It will know no inner tensions between one desire and another, each pulling against the other, nor will desire to do something ever outrun energy and ability to do it. Nor, when we are in glory, shall we ever lack, or fail to show, love to the Father, the Son, and the Holy Spirit, and to all the brothers and sisters in Christ who are with us there.

This, however, is about as far as we can go.

3. We shall be given a new home life.

Now Paul comes to the climax of the contrast he is draw-
ing between our ongoing life of faith in Christ in this
world and our promised future life of seeing him and
being forever as close to him as can be. He expresses
the contrast, as we have seen, in domestic terms: "away
from the body . . . at home with the Lord" (2 Cor. 5:6, 8).
While still in this body—away; but when away from this
body—home. Jesus himself assured his first disciples, "I
go to prepare a place for you . . . I will come again and
will take you to myself, that where I am you may be also"
(John 14:2–3). Those disciples represented all the believers that ever would be, and Jesus's promise is a word to
each one of us.

Similarly, when he prayed, "Father, I desire that they
also, whom you have given me, may be with me where
I am, to see my glory" (John 17:24), he was praying for
you and me, and for all the believers of all time. Every
day every Christian may, and surely should, renew his or
her grip on the promise and the prayer, take a long look
ahead, and say with Paul, "Yes, we are of good courage,

and we would rather be away from the body and at home with Lord" (2 Cor. 5:8).

Look Forward, and Look to Christ

What I have had to say about weakness being the way in the Christian life has now been said. Men and women of the world draw on their talents and ingenuity to map out for themselves paths of strength and success in worldly terms. Christians plan paths of faithfulness to Christ knowing that these involve both apparent and real weakness. And they settle for this on the understanding that journeyings of faithfulness, which please their Lord as of now, lead to final glories.

Neither I who write these pages nor anyone who reads them knows as yet what it will be like, experientially, to leave this world. But one day we shall all have to do that, and it is wonderful to know that somewhere in the process of transition out of the body into the next world, Christ himself will meet us, so that we may expect his face to be the first thing we become aware of in that new order of life into which we will have moved. Looking forward to this is the hope that will sustain us, as evidently it sustained Paul, while we grow older and our weaknesses, limitations, and thorns in the flesh increase. "So we are always of good courage" (2 Cor. 5:6). May it ever be so.

Meantime, the path that we tread daily is overshadowed—no, the appropriate wording is *lit up*—by Christ himself, our Savior and Lord, who in alliance with the Holy Spirit indwelling us really though invisibly walks beside us all the way. He, our sin-bearing Mediator with the Father, is our shepherd, guide, and model. He is the source of our strength in weakness and of our hope of heaven. He sustains us when our life and well-being are under threat, and his redemptive self-giving for us teaches us generosity in financial giving to relieve others' needs, one way in which we express our gratitude for grace. Such are the aspects of what is sometimes called the all-sufficiency of Christ that 2 Corinthians displays. For Paul, the Lord Jesus is the controlling center of life in every respect, being both example and enabler throughout.

So it is no wonder that Paul in his sign-off prayer puts the Lord Jesus first in the holy Trinitarian team of the three persons who are the one God. "The grace of the Lord Jesus Christ and the love of God and the fellowship"—the shared life—"of the Holy Spirit be with you all" (13:14). And that is my prayer also as I bring this book to a close.

General Index

Scripture Index

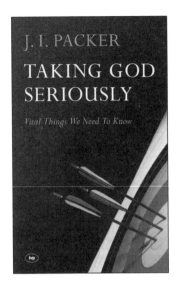

also by J. I. Packer

Taking God Seriously
Vital things we need to know
J. I. Packer

ISBN: 978-1-84474-609-5
176 pages, paperback

Catechesis consists of intentional, orderly instruction in the truths by which Christians are called to live – a sort of discipleship in 'mere Christianity'.

The fact that catechesis has fallen out of the life and practice of many churches today is a major loss, leaving Christians undernourished and spiritually sluggish. Professor J. I. Packer responds that 'it is catechesis – vital ongoing teaching and discipling – that hits the bull's eye': it is of the utmost importance in developing a church that maintains orthodox beliefs.

Packer urges Christians to know their faith so they can explain it to inquirers, sustain it against sceptics, and put it to work in evangelism, church fellowship, and the many forms of service – this is the Christian's business of taking God seriously.

'Dr Packer has the rare ability to deal with profound and basic spiritual truths in a practical and highly readable way.'
Billy Graham

Available from your local Christian bookshop or **www.thinkivp.com**

Inter-Varsity Press

For more information about IVP
and our publications visit
www.ivpbooks.com

Get regular updates at **ivpbooks.com/signup**
Find us on **facebook.com/ivpbooks**
Follow us on **twitter.com/ivpbookcentre**

Inter-Varsity Press, a company limited by guarantee registered in England and Wales, number 05202650. Registered office IVP Bookcentre, Norton Street, Nottingham NG7 3HR, United Kingdom. Registered charity number 1105757.